Gross Me Out!

50 Nasty Projects to Disgust Your Friends & Repulse Your Family

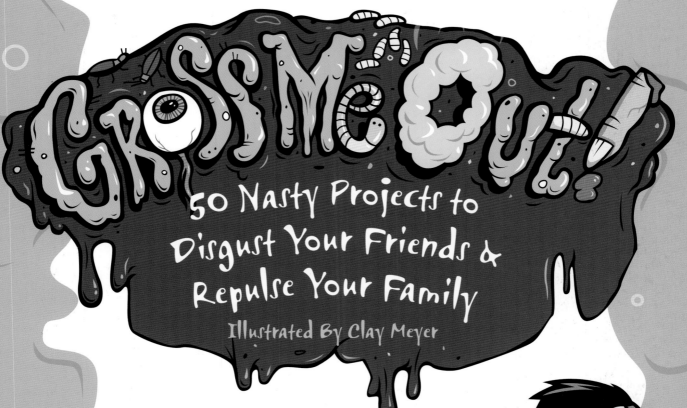

Gross Me Out!

50 Nasty Projects to Disgust Your Friends & Repulse Your Family

Illustrated By Clay Meyer

LARK BOOKS

A Division of Sterling Publishing Co., Inc.
New York

Authors
Sloppy Joe Rhatigan
Revoltin' Rain Newcomb

Illustrator & Cover Illustrator
Clay "Munching Maggots" Meyer

Art Director
Slime-Time Stacey Budge

Cover Designer
Barfin' Barbara Zaretsky

Production Assistance
Shannon "Yucky" Yokeley
Lougie Laura Gabris

Editorial Assistance
Delores "Pull My Finger" Gosnell

The Library of Congress has cataloged the hardcover edition as follows:

Rhatigan, Joe.
  Gross me out! : 50 nasty projects to disgust your friends & repulse your family / [authors, Joe Rhatigan & Rain Newcomb] ; illustrated by Clay Meyer.
      p. cm.
  Includes index.
  Summary: A collection of fifty experiments and activities for "awesomely gross" things to do or make, including fake blood, roadkill roast, and slime games.
  ISBN 1-57990-505-6
  1. Science--Experiments--Juvenile literature. 2. Scientific recreations--Juvenile literature. [1. Science--Experiments. 2. Experiments. 3. Scientific recreations.] I. Newcomb, Rain. II. Meyer, Clay, ill. III. Title.
Q164.R48 2004
793.8--dc22
                                                                2003022027

10 9 8 7 6 5 4 3 2

Published by Lark Books, a division of
Sterling Publishing Co., Inc.
387 Park Avenue South, New York, NY 10016

First Paperback Edition 2005
© 2004, Lark Books
© 2004, Illustrations, Clay Meyer

Distributed in Canada by Sterling Publishing,
c/o Canadian Manda Group, 165 Dufferin Street
Toronto, Ontario, Canada M6K 3H6

Distributed in the United Kingdom by GMC Distribution Services,
Castle Place, 166 High Street, Lewes, East Sussex, England BN7 1XU

Distributed in Australia by Capricorn Link (Australia) Pty Ltd.,
P.O. Box 704, Windsor, NSW 2756 Australia

If you have questions or comments about this book, please contact:
Lark Books, 67 Broadway, Asheville, NC 28801, (828) 253-0467

Manufactured in China
All rights reserved

ISBN 13: 978-1-57990-505-7 (hardcover) 978-1-57990-752-5 (paperback)
ISBN 10: 1-57990-505-6 (hardcover) 1-57990-752-0 (paperback)

For information about custom editions, special sales, premium and corporate purchases, please contact Sterling Special Sales Department at 800-805-5489 or specialsales@

Dedication

For my mom, who cleaned up all my gross stuff growing up, and did it with love.

--CM

To Kayleigh, Evan, and Maggie, for all the poopy diapers, booger balls, regurgitated baby food, and disgusting objects found outside. Gross picnics wouldn't be the same without you!

--JR

To Jon, who brings a whole new level of meaning to the concept of fart math, and Ben, the grossest person I know.

--RN

Contents

Hey! I'm Ralph and this is Betty Lou!

Gross Greetings!

Some people think the whole caterpillar to butterfly transformation is a beautiful thing to behold. Forget beautiful butterflies, I say, give me DUNG BEETLES. I mean, here is a bug that lives in, eats, and rolls perfectly round pieces of POOP. Why? Why not! And right off the bat, I want to dedicate this book to all dung beetles great and small, and the beautiful poop balls they make. I mean, the ancient Egyptians practically worshipped dung beetles, and they were some pretty smart people. They built those pyramid thingys, didn't they!?

So what does this book have to do with dung beetles? Well, nothing really, except that rolling poop balls for a living is gross and so are the 50 activities and projects in this book.

My name is Ralph Retcher, and me and my best friend Betty Lou Goo will take you through some awesomely gross things to do and make. Every now and then, you'll also hear from my next door neighbor Frederico Farkus. He's smart; although, to me, he doesn't seem very gross.

This book explores absolutely everything that's gross. First, we'll figure out just how disgusting our bodies are with a whole bunch of fun experiments, projects, and sickening things to do. Then, we'll visit Gross Grandma in her kitchen and sample some of her repugnant recipes. Yummy! Can't wait! We've also gathered a perfectly horrid collection of gifts to make for the people who love us and love to be grossed out. And, we'll even put on our adventure clothes (if we can find them under our beds) and explore the gross outdoors. Finally, the last chapter (our favorite) celebrates how gross you've become just by reading this book.

Have fun, and get ready for a disgusting dose of gross!

I'm Fredericho Farkus III. Let me formally introduce you to our book.

CHAPTER ONE

Your Very Gross Body

Yeah, yeah, sure everyone tells you how interesting your body is, but when you get right down to it, most of what your body does, smells like, and produces, is GROSS. Take toe jam for instance. You wake up in the morning, bathe like most other humans, put on a pair of socks and your sneakers. By the end of the day you've got JAM between your toes. Where'd that stuff come from anyway!? I had socks and sandals on, for gosh sakes, and all of a sudden I've got jam between my toes. Cool. These projects and activities are great for figuring out just how disgusting your body can be.

Body Critters

What lives in your mouth, on your hands, in your ears, in between your toes, in your nose, under your pits? Microscopic critters, of course. Try this activity and find out just what these little critters look like.

what you need

Water
Measuring cup
Saucepan
Use of a stove
Chicken or beef
   boullion cube
Sugar

Tablespoon
Jar lids (they must
   be very clean)
   or petri dishes*
Cotton swabs
Rubber gloves
Plastic wrap

*Petri dishes are available at science supply stores and in many stores that sell school supplies.

Get an adult to help you with this project!

what you do

1 To make some yummy bacteria food, bring 1 cup of water to a boil in the saucepan.

2 Add the boullion cube and 1 tablespoon of sugar to the boiling water. Stir until it's completely dissolved.

3 Carefully pour the mixture into each lid or petri dish, filling them about halfway.

4 While the mixture cools, decide where you'd like to collect bacteria from. How about your armpits, between your toes, your hands, or your tongue?

5 Put on the rubber gloves, and use a cotton swab to take a sample from a body part. (The rubber gloves will keep the bacteria on your hands from mixing with the bacteria in between your toes or wherever.) After you collect a sample, put the cotton swab in a lid or petri dish. Repeat with other places on your body, using a new swab each time.

6 Cover the jar lids or petri dishes with the plastic wrap and put them in a warm place. Check back in a week or so to see what sort of bacteria your body is hosting.

Hallelujah Halitosis

Class, everybody's got breath, right!? It's up to you to make sure yours smells bad. Not sure if yours is odiferous? Here are three easy ways to find out:

1 Walk up to your teacher and say, "Hhhhhhhhh."

2 Floss your back teeth and smell the floss.

3 Scrape the farthest back area of your tongue with a wash cloth, wait 45 seconds, and smell the wash cloth.

Halitosis and Cheese Sandwich

If your breath doesn't pass the stink test, make yourself this delicious snack.

what you need

Wheat bread (2 pieces)
Hummus
Tuna fish
Fresh onions
Limburger cheese

what you do

1 Slather the hummus onto the bread.

2 Sprinkle the fresh onions onto the middle of the sandwich.

3 Cut the cheese. Ha ha ha.

4 Place the cheese and tuna on the sandwich and eat away.

5 Find someone to breathe on.

Poop Soap

Just because you have to be clean every now and then, doesn't mean you can't be gross about it. Make a soap that looks like poop just to make your point.

what you need

Wax paper
2 tablespoons of glycerin*
1 heaping tablespoon of cornstarch (plus a little extra)
Measuring spoons
Small glass bowl
4 ounces white glycerin soap base (also known
    as melt-and-pour soap)**
Knife and cutting board
Measuring cup or other microwave-safe container
Microwave oven
Brown soap coloring**
Large metal spoon

*Available at drugstores
**Available at the soapmaking supply department of craft stores

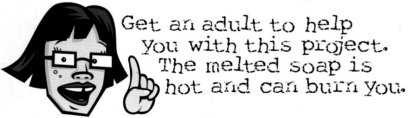

Get an adult to help you with this project. The melted soap is hot and can burn you.

what you do

1 Cover where you're working with wax paper. Melted soap can be a bit messy if you're not careful.

2 Mix together the glycerin and 1 heaping tablespoon of cornstarch in the bowl. (Continued on page 18.)

What makes poop smell, anyway?

Good question, Betty Lou. Poop is mostly water, and the rest is food your body can't digest, known as fiber. The dead bacteria that live in your intestines and help you digest your food are also included in this nice package, and it's these microscopic corpses that make your poop smell. You see, bacteria make sulfur, the stuff that gives eggs (especially rotten ones) their odor. And boy, do they smell like poop. Or should I say, poop smells like them.

Poop Soap continued

3 Sprinkle a sheet of wax paper with some more cornstarch, and set it aside.

4 With the knife, cut the soap base into ½-inch cubes. Put the cubes in the measuring cup. Melt the soap in the microwave on high for 30 seconds. Have your adult helper check to make sure the soap is completely melted. Don't let the soap boil.

5 Once the soap is melted (be careful, it's pretty hot), remove it from the microwave. When the soap stops steaming, add a couple drops of the brown coloring, and stir with the large metal spoon. If the soap is not nice and poopy brown, add a couple more drops. Note: If you add too much coloring, the soap may stain. Also, don't use food coloring or coloring used for candles.

6 Once the soap has stopped steaming, have the adult pour the melted soap into the cornstarch mixture. Stir. When the soap starts to harden, pick it up out of the bowl and place it on the sheet of wax paper.

7 Coat your hands with cornstarch, and knead the soap until it's smooth.

8 Mold the soap into one big poop, and let it harden.

Gardyloo!
Here Comes the Poo!

Back in the old days, if you heard someone yell, "Gardyloo," you either ran for cover or quickly opened up your umbrella. I know what you're guessing, but "gardyloo" doesn't mean, "It's about to rain." Way back in the 1800s, people didn't have indoor plumbing, and folks in the city didn't have room for outhouses. What did they do? They pooped and peed in little bowls they kept in their bedrooms (called chamber pots). Did the pee and poop magically disappear? Of course not. People simply threw it out the window onto the road below. If the poop and pee tosser was up a couple of stories, he or she wouldn't yell, "Watch out, I'm throwing a bunch of poop and pee out the window!" Not only did it take too long to say, but it was sort of embarrassing. They simply yelled "Gardyloo!" Simple? Yes. Healthy? Not so much. Ever heard of the disease cholera? All cholera needed to spread and infect thousands of people was a little too much gardylooing.

Fart Math

The average person farts 14 times a day. Are you average or above average? Let's find out, shall we?

what you need

Pen and paper
Calculator (optional)

what you do

1 Carry the pen and paper around with you all day long. Each time you fart, record the time of the explosion in your notebook.

2 Do this for three days.

3 To find the average number of times you fart per day, add the number of farts from each day together. Divide that number by three (the number of days you counted farts). The result is the average number of times you fart per day.

4 As well as recording the number of times per day you farted, record exactly what you ate and when you ate it. Can you find a connection between diet and flatulence? (Flatulence is a big word for a big stink!)

5 After you figure out whether or not you're above average, spend the day with Gross Grandma, and figure out her fart factor. The good news is, you fart more the older you get!

FRRRRRRRTTT!!

Get the Most Out of Your Farts!

1 Eat "fart food," such as wheat, milk, cheese, butter, cabbage, apples, radishes, broccoli, onions, cauliflower, Brussels sprouts, and beans. (Although perhaps not all at the same time.)

2 Drink carbonated beverages. It's not the carbonation that makes you fart though, it's the bacteria munching on the fructose in your intestines.

3 Drink through a straw. You'll swallow air as you do. The air will either come out one end (burp) or the other (toot).

4 Eat quickly. This will trap air in your belly, just like drinking through a straw.

5 Chew gum. You swallow air when you chew gum, too.

6 To make your farts louder, always make sure you're sitting down when one comes down the pike.

Bogus Blood

It looks like blood, but it tastes like dessert! Mix up a batch of fake blood, smear it on your arm, show off your boo boo to your friends, and then...lick it off!

what you need

Measuring cup and spoons
½ cup light corn syrup
2 tablespoons creamy peanut butter
2 tablespoons chocolate syrup
Mixing bowl
Wire whisk
  20 drops red food coloring

what you do

1 Put everything but the food coloring into the bowl. Stir them together with the whisk until you have a smooth, creamy mixture.

2 Add the food coloring to the mixture and stir it some more.

Be careful, young man; that fake blood will stain clothing, tablecloths, walls, and even some countertops.

Fake Scabs

Whoever said, "No pain, no gain" obviously didn't know how to make a good-looking fake scab.

what you need

Measuring spoons
White craft glue
6 drops red food coloring and 1 drop green food coloring
Small dish or bowl
Craft stick
Toothpick (optional)
Blow-dryer (optional)

what you do

1 Put 1 teaspoon of the white craft glue and the food coloring in the bowl. Mix it all together with the craft stick.

2 Apply the mixture to your skin with the craft stick. The thicker the scab mixture, the thicker and more disgusting-looking the scab will be. Thicker scabs take longer to dry. The mixture will wrinkle as it dries, adding to the scab effect.

3 If you want to make stitches or a smaller wound, use the tip of a toothpick. You can use a blow-dryer set on low heat to speed up the drying time.

Poo-tiful Facial

It's amazing what kinds of horrid goop you can put on somebody's face if you tell them it's good for their skin!

what you need

Sliced potato or cucumber
Someone to experiment on
Stuff from your kitchen
Camera (optional)

what you do

1 Put a slice of potato or cucumber over each eye of the person you'll be experimenting on. Then your victim—I mean friend—won't know what kind of horrid concoction she's being smeared with.

2 Smear any of the mashed items or the plain yogurt on your friend's face. Leave it on for a few minutes. Take a picture if you want. Then rinse it off.

3 If you're using the egg white or mayonnaise, spread it on your friend's face and leave it on for 20 minutes. (Tie your friend up, if necessary.) Take a picture and rinse it off.

Poo-tiful Concoctions

- **Mash grapes into a thick paste with apple juice.**
- **Blend avocados and bananas into a finely mashed mix.**
- **Mash up some tomatoes.**
- **Use plain yogurt straight from the fridge (no need to mash).**
- **Beat an egg white with an electric mixer until it's stiff.**
- **How about mayonnaise and other condiments?**

Battle Boredom with Disgusting Things to Do

You don't have to wait for a rainy day to try out any or all of these amazing nasty things you can do with little or no effort.

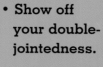

- Make rude farting sounds by pressing your lips to a body part and blowing. Try your arm, hands, umm…is there anywhere else you can reach?

- Blow spit bubbles.

- Show people the whites of your eyes.

- Turn your top eyelid inside out.

- Crack your knuckles.

- Hawk a fake lougie. A lougie is a cross between snot and spit. Make a noise as if you're trying to get snot out from your throat, and then, pretend to spit and blow hard into someone's hair.

- If you're really talented, you can pick your nose with your tongue.

- Show off your double-jointedness.

  - Bite your toenails— but only in public.

- Sure you can cup your hand under a pit and flap your arm until a nice fart noise comes out, but can you do hand farts? What about behind the knee farts? Keep trying.

- Put fake dandruff (cornstarch, instant oatmeal, etc.) in your hair and scratch it out in front of people.

- Make younger siblings pull your finger, and then fart. Little kids always fall for this one!

- Hold a burping contest. Each contestant burps as many letters in the alphabet as they can. Remember the letter everyone ends on. The person who makes it furthest through the alphabet wins!

Not Snot

Make 'em and flick 'em.

what you need

Measuring cup
Laundry booster*
1 quart soda bottle with cap (clean and empty)
Warm water
Bowl

White craft glue
Craft stick
Green food coloring
Tablespoon

* Borax brand works great.

what you do

1 Put ½ cup of the laundry booster in the soda bottle. Fill the bottle with warm water. Screw on the lid, and shake it until almost all of the booster has dissolved.

2 In the bowl, mix together ½ cup of the craft glue and ½ cup of water. Stir it with the craft stick.

3 Add 2 drops of the green food coloring to the glue and water. Mix it together. Add more food coloring if your boogers needs to be greener.

4 Pour 8 tablespoons of the booster solution into the booger bowl. Stir it up until it gets clumpy. (If the snot is too runny, add a little more of the booster solution.)

5 Take the boogers out of the bowl. Use them for all sorts of evil purposes.

Got Snot?

Snot really isn't THAT repulsive…I mean, it's just water, salt, and a little protein spewing out of your nose faster than a herd of galloping horses. Your body can make enough mucus in a single day to fill four glasses (that's about a quart of snot), and you swallow about half of that every day. Normally, your snot is perfectly clear. Dead bacteria mixed up in it make it a whole rainbow of colors though. If you're sick and your nose is full of mucus and viruses, things get downright disgusting and dangerous. Some snot-born germs can float around for an hour or more!

Inflamed, Infected, Lesion Fun

Re-create a pus-filled pustule, a festering sore, a bleeding blister, or even a pulsating pimple with this model that really oozes. Almost as good as the real thing!

what you need

Small glass or plastic bottle
  with narrow neck
Piece of cardboard about
  12 x 15 inches
Modeling clay
Funnel or piece of heavy
  paper to roll into a funnel

Measuring cup
1 pound box of bicarbonate
  of soda (baking soda)
Yellow food coloring
1 quart bottle of vinegar
Spoon
Plastic or newspaper

what you do

1 Stand the bottle in the middle of the cardboard.

2 Create a sore or blister around the bottle with the modeling clay. Leave the mouth of the bottle partially open.

3 Use the funnel to fill the bottle about halfway with baking soda.

4 Pour a few drops of yellow food coloring into ½ cup of vinegar, and stir it.

5 Cover a table with the plastic or newspaper. Place the sore on the table. Carefully pour some of the yellow vinegar into the opening in the sore. Stand back! It's about to fester! It's gonna blow! Every time it stops oozing, pour more vinegar into the sore.

Oozing Brain Salad

Hey, this is edible, but it looks better than it tastes.

what you need

Small bowl (about the size of the top of your head)
Aluminum foil
Cooking spray
Water
Large pot
6 ounces spaghetti
Small saucepan
Measuring cup

1 packet unflavored gelatin
Spoon
½ cup of crushed ice
Colander
Gray cake-decorating dye
Plastic wrap
Large plate
1 jar pasta sauce

what you do

1 Make the inside of the small bowl more brain-like by adding wads of foil along the sides of the bowl. The inside of the bowl will be more egg-shaped than round.

2 Line the bowl with a large sheet of the foil (cover the entire interior of the bowl including the tinfoil wads). Press the foil gently to create a skull-shaped cavity. Spray it generously with the cooking spray.

3 Bring the water to a boil in the large pot. Break the dry spaghetti into 3- to 4-inch pieces, and add it to the boiling water. Cook it according to the package directions, usually about eight to 10 minutes, or until the spaghetti is tender.

4 While the spaghetti is cooking, boil ½ cup of water in the saucepan. Remove it from the heat, and stir in one packet of unflavored gelatin. Stir until the gelatin is completely dissolved. Then stir in ½ cup of crushed ice.

5 When the spaghetti is done, drain it into the colander, and return it to the cooking pot. Add the gray cake-decorating dye one drop at a time. Stir it into the pasta well until it's a very pale gray color. (Brains are very pale gray, so you don't need much dye at all.)

6 When the gelatin is slightly congealed, add the pasta and stir it well.

7 Pour the entire mix into the prepared mold.

8 Cover the mold with plastic wrap, and refrigerate until it forms a gelatinous blob.

9 To unmold, remove the plastic wrap, and cover the bowl with a large plate. Holding the plate pon top of the bowl, flip the bowl and plate over in one motion, so that the plate is on the bottom. Carefully remove the bowl and foil.

10 Spoon warmed pasta sauce around the sides of the brain. Eat it if you dare.

Now That's Entertainment!

Forget the Corny Clown, the Singing Cowboy, or the mealy-mouthed Magician. If you want to entertain your guests at your next party, stage a do-it-yourself autopsy. Yes, a real, live, pretend autopsy.

what you need

Table
String
Tacks
Old sheet
Scissors
Tomatoes
Grapes
Uncooked liver
Pet hair
Rubber glove
Gelatin
Dried apricot

Pickle
Cooked spaghetti
Some shoeboxes, plastic
  containers, or other
  containers
A willing accomplice
Desk lamp
Lab coat (if you've got
  one handy)
Drill (if you've got
  one handy)

what you do

1 Set up the table where you'll put on your show. Use the tacks to hang the string above the table so that when you hang the sheet over the string, the sheet is in front of the table and covers up what you're doing behind the sheet.

2 Cut a slit in the sheet big enough for a few hands to fit through.

3 Prepare the body parts: peel the tomatoes, squash them a little. These are the brains. Peel then freeze the grapes.

These are the eyeballs. Place the liver in a container. This is the liver. Comb a dog or cat, and pull the hair from the comb. This is the hair. Prepare the gelatin, and pour it in the glove. Tie the glove, and put in the refrigerator to set. That's a hand. The dried apricot is an ear, the pickle a nose, and the spaghetti is the pack of worms you found in the body. Place all the body parts in containers.

4 When you're ready to entertain your guests, turn off the lights, have your accomplice lie on the table, and set up the desk lamp so they can see your shadow on the sheet.

5 Gather your guests, and start your story. If you've got a lab coat, put it on. The story can go something like this: Guests, thank you for coming. I'd like to perform an autopsy for you. I found this body in the woods a few weeks back, and it has been under my bed waiting just for this opportunity. You will not be able to see what I'm doing behind this sheet; however, you'll be able to feel the body parts once I've extracted them from the body.

6 Go behind the sheet, make a bunch of noise, and pretend you're working on your assistant's head. If you've got a drill handy, turn it on for some good sound effects. Put the squishy tomatoes just below the slit you made in the sheet. Ask your guests to put their hands through the slit, and tell them they're feeling your body's brains! Do the same thing for the rest of the body parts. Use the drill when you can, and have fun!

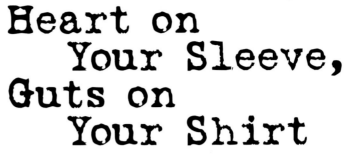

Heart on Your Sleeve, Guts on Your Shirt

These shirts will be the hit of the party. Wear them everywhere.

what you need

White or brightly
   colored T-shirt
Internet access
Inkjet printer
Iron-on transfer paper*
Iron

*Available at craft stores

what you do

1 Go online and find a picture of what your heart or guts look like. Try online medical libraries and doctors' resources.

2 Print the images you find onto the iron-on transfer paper.

3 Place the clean T-shirt on top of a hard surface such as a countertop.

4 Place the image facedown over the shirt. Iron over the image, following the directions from the iron-on transfer paper.

CHAPTER TWO

Gross Grandma's Repugnant Recipes

Hello. Why, aren't you sweet. It's so hard these days to find good food you kiddies will eat. Food can be such a bore. I mean, a peanut butter and jelly sandwich makes me yawn. However, if you squash the sandwich and mold it into the shape of an ear, then you've really got something you can sink your teeth into. Ralph, Betty, and Frederico have invited me to include several of my delectable and disgusting recipes in their wonderful new book. So, get out to the gross-ery store and pick up the ingredients for these awesome recipes. Tell them Gross Grandma sent you.

Get a gross adult to help you with these recipes.

Toe Jam Dip

Sure, you probably eat your own toe jam anyway, which is terribly gross and not at all good for you; however, if you don't have enough toe jam to share with everybody, here's a great recipe for making more.

what you need

Small bowl
1 small box vanilla instant
  pudding mix
¾ cup milk
½ cup sour cream
¼ cup cottage cheese
8-ounce can crushed
  pineapple (undrained)

½ cup flaked coconut
Yellow food coloring
6 to 8 green and red apples
Knife
Vegetable peeler
Platter

what you do

1 In a small bowl, mix together the vanilla pudding mix, milk, sour cream, cottage cheese, crushed pineapple, and coconut.

2 Add a few drops of yellow food coloring to make it look kind of like pus. Set the toe jam dip aside.

3 Core the apples, and cut each of them into wedges.

4 Have an adult help you carve the top of the apple wedges with the knife to make them look like the end of your big toe.

5 Use the vegetable peeler to remove the peel from the apples, leaving a little "toenail" shaped peel at the end.

6 Place the bowl of toe jam on a large platter and surround it with the big toe apple wedges.

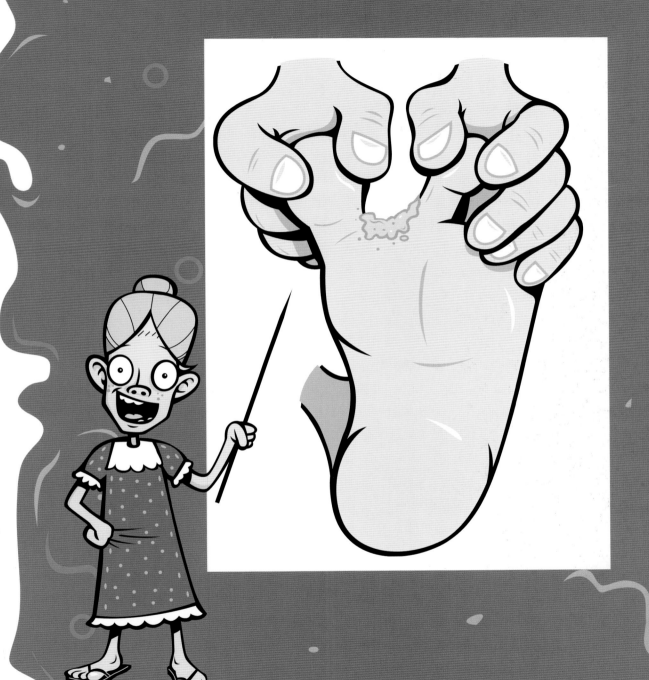

Curdled Milk Pancreas with Green Salsa Bile

I only take this recipe out for special occasions such as holidays, birthdays, or whenever I visit a sick neighbor.

what you need

1 gallon of milk
Large pot
Red and orange food coloring
2 tablespoons of lemon juice
Measuring spoons

Long-handled wooden spoon
Colander
Cheesecloth
Salsa verde (green salsa)

what you do

1 Pour the milk into a large pot. Add 2 drops each of the red and orange food coloring so that the milk is slightly pinkish-orange and kind of fleshy looking.

2 Bring the milk to a boil.

3 When the milk begins to boil, turn off the burner, add the lemon juice, and stir it. The milk will start to curdle.

4 Line the colander with several layers of cheesecloth. Use several long pieces so that the cheesecloth hangs over the edge of the colander.

5 Carefully pour the curdled milk into the cheesecloth-lined colander. Allow it to drain and cool for a few minutes.

6 When the curdled milk has cooled enough to handle, gather the edges of the cheesecloth, and give the mass a good squeeze to remove some of the remaining liquid. Keep the curdled milk covered with the cheesecloth as you mold it into a pancreas shape.

7 Place the pancreas-shaped curdled milk back into the colander, place the colander in a pot, and put the whole thing into the fridge. Let it drain for three or four hours.

8 Before serving, spoon globs of bile (salsa verde) onto a medium-sized plate. Remove the cheesecloth from the curdled milk pancreas, and place it in the center of the bile.

Bug Buffet

Yes! We're talking about eating insects! As I said before, kids won't eat hardly anything these days; however, as soon as a simple schoolyard double dog dare is issued, these same kids who won't touch Mom's meat loaf are eating BUGS. So, forget the double dare, and try these delicious buggy recipes.

Don't cook bugs unless you have an adult helping you.

what you need

Coffee can with plastic lid
Scissors
Bug net

Several grasshoppers
  or crickets
Baking sheet
Aluminum foil

what you do

1 First you have to find yourself some crispy critters. Grasshoppers and crickets are a great place to start. Cut an X in the center of the plastic coffee lid. This will allow you to catch the insects and push them in the can without them jumping out. Now, look in tall grass, woodpiles, or under rocks.

2 Place your can of bugs into your freezer for an hour or two. This will knock them out. Take the bugs out of the freezer and rinse them well in warm water. Now they're ready to dry roast.

3 Roast your insects on a foil-covered baking sheet for one to two hours at 200°F. Insects are done when they're crispy and you can crush them with a spoon. Once roasted, remove the legs and wings. You can eat them as is, or dip them in your favorite sauce. For chocolate-covered crickets, melt two squares of semisweet chocolate in a bowl, dip your roasted insects in the chocolate, and let them cool.

Critter Fritters

If you don't want to roast your critters, fry 'em!

what you need

½ cup flour
1 teaspoon baking powder
1 teaspoon salt
Measuring cup and spoons
Bowl
Spoon
1½ cups milk

1 egg
1 cup stunned and rinsed
   grasshoppers (not yet
   dry roasted)
Cooking oil
Frying pan

what you do

1 Mix the flour, baking powder, and salt together in a bowl. Slowly add the milk, and beat until smooth.

2 Add the egg, and beat well. Remove the grasshoppers' wings and legs. Dip them into the batter, and fry in oil until crispy.

3 Salt and serve.

Gross Food People Eat on Purpose

You think processed cheese in a can is gross? How about mayonnaise? Well, these foods are nothing compared to some of the disgusting foods out there.

HAGGIS: If you go to Scotland, you might be able to eat some of the grossest grub ever. Haggis is made by stuffing the stomach of a dead sheep with its internal organs (heart, liver, lungs, and kidneys), all chopped up. Add some suet (that's the hard, white fat around the kidneys), a little oatmeal, and simmer the stuffed stomach for four hours.

HEADCHEESE: There's no cheese in headcheese, but there is a lot of head. Headcheese is made from a cow or pig's head. First, cut off the cheeks, forehead, and nose. Wrap them tightly in a piece of cloth and boil them for hours. It will turn into a clear, gelatinous soup with chunks of meat floating in it. Chill the headcheese until it hardens, then spread it on bread.

SWEETBREADS: Like headcheese, there's nothing sweet or breadlike in it. Sweetbread is the thymus gland of a young cow.

Colombians munch on roasted ants instead of popcorn at movie theaters.

Here are some other gross treats from around the world: jellied blood, pickled chicken feet, jellied eels, escargot (garden snails), fish eyes (don't forget to spit out the cornea), fish head soup, rancid yak milk, and last but not least, gelatin: that wonderful jiggly dessert, which is made from the bones, skins, hooves, and tendons of cows and other animals. Yummy!

Gangrene Fingers with Bloody Stump Sauce

Now here's some finger food you can really sink your teeth into.

what you need

Small glass bowl
Spoon
1 small jar of plum sauce
Red food coloring
Medium bowl
1-pound package of rollable
    fondant icing*

Green food coloring
Measuring cup
¼ cup sliced almonds
Cookie sheet
Serving plate

*Available in cake-decorating supply
    stores

what you do

1 In the small glass bowl, mix the plum sauce with 2 or 3 drops of the red food coloring. Stir it until the plum sauce looks like blood.

2 In the medium bowl, knead the fondant icing with a few drops of green food coloring. Knead the icing until the green color is totally mixed.

3 Mold about ¼ cup of the icing into a finger. Press one of the sliced almonds onto the end of one of the fondant fingers to make a nail.

4 Place the fingers on a cookie sheet, and let them air dry overnight. Place the bowl of blood plum sauce in the middle of the serving plate. Arrange the fingers around the plate.

Vile Bile

Also known as Barf Fondue, this scrumptious appetizer will remind you and your friends of all the times you've been sick enough to spew your guts out.

what you need

½ cup canned black beans
Spoon
8-ounce jar queso dip
½ cup canned diced
   tomatoes with cilantro
   and garlic

¼ cup canned corn, drained
2 thinly sliced scallions
Measuring cup
Glass bowl
Warm bread, chips,
   or veggies

what you do

1 With the back of a spoon, slightly smash the black beans.

2 Place the queso dip, corn, black beans, scallions, and diced tomatoes into the glass bowl, and mix thoroughly.

3 Heat the mixture in the microwave for two to three minutes. Stop the microwave and stir the fondue once every minute.

4 Serve the barf fondue warm with bread, chips, or veggies.

As you ingest your yummy vomit treat, let's talk about what's really in vomit. We've got semi-digested food, spit, and stomach acid. And if your puke is green, your body threw some bile in for kicks. Bile is a chemical from down in your gallbladder and intestines, which means that was where your upchucked food came from.

Vomit Thesaurus

Although vomiting is never fun while it's happening, talking about it afterwards is great! Here are several different names you could call the act of puking or puke itself (in alphabetical order for your convenience):

Barf
Blow Bile
Blow Chunks
Blow Your Cookies
Boot Camp
Call Ralph on the Big White Telephone
Chowder
Chum
Deliver a Pavement Pizza
Heave
Hock Up a Furball
Hork
Huey
Hug the Porcelain Wishing Well
Hurl
Lose Your Lunch
Puke
Regurgitate
Reverse Diarrhea
Round-Trip Meal Ticket
Shaq-Fu
Shout at Your Shoes
Sneeze Cheese
Spew

Spill the Groceries
Split Pea Spew
Technicolor Yawn
Toss Your Cookies
Toss Your Tacos
Upchuck
Woof
Yak
Yark
Yeech
Yodel

Make Up Your Own Fun Terms:
_____
_____
_____
_____

Deer Droppings

Drop these bite-sized poop pellets into your lunchbox. Make sure you have enough for everyone.

what you need

Baking pan
Aluminum foil
Vegetable spray
  Small bowl
   Measuring cup
    and spoons
   2 tablespoons
    cocoa powder
1 cup plus 3 tablespoons
  powdered sugar

1 cup sugar
1 cup light corn syrup
2 saucepans
Spoon
¾ cup water
1 package powdered
  fruit pectin*

*Found in the canning supplies section
of grocery stores

what you do

1 Line the baking pan with the foil, and spray it with a light coat of the vegetable spray.

2 In the small bowl, combine the cocoa with 3 tablespoons of powdered sugar.

3 Heat the sugar and the corn syrup to boiling in a small saucepan over medium-high heat. Stir it constantly until the sugar is dissolved. Drop a small amount of the mixture into very cold water. If it separates into very chewy little balls, it's ready.

4 As you're heating the sugar and corn syrup, boil the water and pectin in another saucepan. Reduce the heat to low.

5 Slowly pour the hot sugar mixture in a thin stream into the pectin mixture, stirring it constantly.

6 Remove the mixture from the heat, and let it cool for one minute. Stir in the cocoa and powdered sugar mix.

7 Pour the mixture into the baking pan. Let it sit at room temperature, uncovered, for 24 hours.

8 Lift the foil from the pan, and remove the foil from the sides. Dip a knife in powdered sugar, and cut the deer droppings into ½-inch squares.

9 Wash and dry your hands well. Coat your impeccably clean hands with powdered sugar. Roll the ½-inch squares between the palms of your hands until they resemble little deer pellets. Try not to overwork them, or they'll get too sticky.

10 Let the deer droppings stand uncovered at room temperature overnight. The powdered sugar will be absorbed into the deer droppings. Store them in an airtight container.

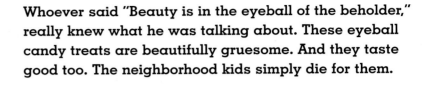

Incredible Edible Eyeballs

Whoever said "Beauty is in the eyeball of the beholder," really knew what he was talking about. These eyeball candy treats are beautifully gruesome. And they taste good too. The neighborhood kids simply die for them.

what you need

1 pound powdered sugar
Sifter
Large bowl
1/3 cup corn syrup
Pinch of salt
1/3 cup softened whipped cream cheese

1 teaspoon almond extract
Measuring cups and spoons
2 small bowls
Black and green food coloring

what you do

1 Sift the powdered sugar into the large bowl. Add the corn syrup, salt, cream cheese, and almond extract. Mix until it's well blended. Add more powdered sugar if the mixture is too sticky. You've now made moldable candy.

2 Place 2 tablespoons of the moldable candy into each of the small bowls. Add 3 to 4 drops of black food color to the candy in one bowl and stir to combine. Add 3 or 4 drops of green to the other bowl and stir well.

3 Roll 1 tablespoon of the uncolored candy into a ball.

4 Make a small patty of green candy, and press it onto the white ball to form the iris.

5 Add a pupil by making an even smaller patty of black candy and pressing it onto the center of the green iris.

6 Repeat with the remaining candy to make the other eye.

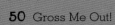

Delectable Diarrhea

This tasty treat reminds me of my last trip overseas. Just remember, when they say, "Don't drink the water," don't.

what you need

1¾ cups cold milk
Box of instant butterscotch
  pudding mix
  Measuring cups and spoons
  Large bowl
  Spoon
    Clear plastic cups
      for serving

1½ cups total of any of the
following ingredients
(a good mix looks the best):
  Almond toffee bits
  Shredded toasted coconut
  Slightly crushed
    vanilla wafers
  Slightly crushed chocolate
    graham crackers
  Mini marshmallows
    cut into bits
  Chopped up peanut brittle
  Diced candy corn
  Diced gummy worms

what you do

1 Pour the milk into the bowl. Add the instant pudding mix, and stir it for two minutes.

2 Add the rest of the ingredients, and stir well.

3 Let the mix sit for about five minutes so that it congeals slightly. Then spoon it into the plastic cups.

4 Serve slightly runny after 10 to 15 minutes, or refrigerate it for two or three hours to serve completely set.

Roadkill Roast

The next time you're at the Roadkill Grill, order this special dish I concocted the night Gross Grandpa ran over our neighbor's pit bull. He wanted pit bull potpie. But this had to do when we realized the poor pooch only suffered minor injuries.

what you need

Cookie sheet
Aluminum foil
Vegetable spray
2 pounds ground turkey
1 cup fresh bread cubes
2 beaten eggs
1 cup finely diced onion
2 cups of tomato sauce
1 package powdered onion
    soup mix

Large bowl
Measuring cup and spoons
2 large handfuls of mung
    bean sprouts
2 pitted black olives
3 tablespoons brown sugar
3 tablespoons orange juice
Small cup
Ketchup
Meat thermometer (optional)

what you do

1 Preheat the oven to 400°F. Line the cookie sheet with the foil, and spray it with a light coat of the vegetable spray.

2 In the large bowl, combine the ground turkey, bread crumbs, eggs, diced onion, 1 cup of the tomato sauce, and the soup mix. Use your very clean hands to squash all the ingredients together.

3 Add the mung bean sprouts, and gently mix them into the meat mixture.

4 Shape the meat loaf into a large ball, and then turn it onto the cookie sheet. Shape the meat into a large armadillo (see illustration), or shape it to resemble some other unfortunate creature. Make a slight indentation on the back to resemble a tire track. Remember, this is road kill; it doesn't have to look like a perfect armadillo shape.

5 Press the olives into the armadillo's face to make eyes. Wash your hands.

6 Place the armadillo in the oven. While it's baking, mix the remaining tomato sauce, brown sugar, and orange juice together in a small cup. Spoon the sauce over the meatloaf every 10 minutes.

7 Bake the armadillo for 40 to 45 minutes, or until a meat thermometer reads 160°F when inserted into the center of the meatloaf.

8 Serve the meatloaf with heated marinade on the side.

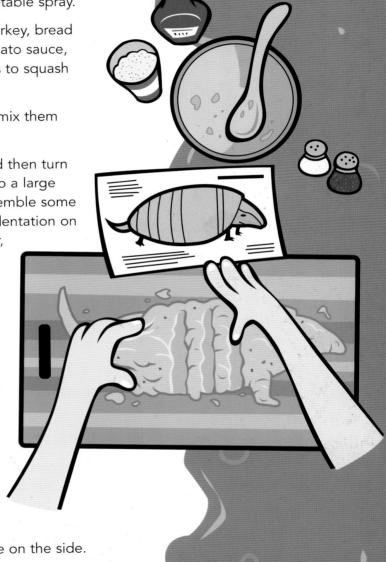

CHAPTER THREE
Gag Gifts

Your parents showcase your toenail collection on the mantel. Your grandparents spoil you rotten with all things rotten. Your friends let you flick THEIR boogers. Your neighbors let you slug hunt in their yard. Your little siblings stink up the joint with their poopy diapers. What a wonderful bunch of people. Repay them with personally handcrafted gifts that will make them gag. They'll be as proud as proud can be. Who wouldn't? I get all choked up just thinking about it. I wonder if I have to hurl.

Slimed!

What's a gross book without slime!? Well, here are three recipes straight from Frederico's secret bedroom laboratory. Slime your friends with gooey goodness.

Super Simple Slime

This is your classic slime recipe. Throw in some plastic flies for extra fun.

what you need

Measuring cups and spoons
Laundry booster*
2 glass containers or bowls
1 cup water
Tablespoon or craft stick
White craft glue

¼ cup water
Self-sealing plastic bags
Food coloring (optional)
Small plastic flies (optional)

*Borax brand works great.

what you do

1 Place 1 tablespoon of the laundry booster into one of the containers. Stir in 1 cup of water until the laundry booster is completely dissolved.

2 Mix together ¼ cup each of glue and water in the other container.

3 In the self-sealing plastic bag, place equal parts of the laundry booster solution and the glue solution. Add food coloring and the flies if you want.

4 Zip up the bag, and knead the mixture. You've got slime! What a great gift. Tell whomever you're giving the gift to that the slime must go back in the bag (or other airtight container) when finished, otherwise it will dry out.

(Slime on over to page 58 for more.)

The Slime goes on...

The Slimiest Slime Ever

You don't even need to add food coloring to this recipe.
It turns a gross yellowish green.

what you need

Measuring cups and spoons   Water
2 glass containers   Laundry booster
Guar gum*   *Available at health food stores

what you do

1 Stir ¼ teaspoon of guar gum into ¼ cup of warm water.

2 Place about 1 cup of water in the second container. Add enough laundry booster to the water so that even after stirring, there's still laundry booster at the bottom of the container.

3 Add about ½ teaspoon of the laundry booster solution to the guar gum solution, and mix. If the mixture is too watery, add a little more laundry booster solution.

The Can't-Find-Laundry-Booster Slimey Slime

This version is rather runny and sticky, but it works!

what you need

White craft glue   Craft stick
Tablespoon   Liquid starch
Paper cup   Small plastic flies (optional)
Food coloring (optional)

what you do

1 Put 2 tablespoons of the white craft glue in the paper cup. Add 1 or 2 drops of the food coloring, and stir it with the craft stick.

2 Add 1 tablespoon of the liquid starch to the paper cup. Stir until it's mixed in.

3 Take the slime out of the paper cup, and knead it until it has the proper consistency.

Other Variations

• Follow the Super Simple Slime instructions, and add 1 tablespoon of chalk or plaster of paris.

• Follow the Super Simple Slime instructions, and add 1 teaspoon of talcum powder and about 2 teaspoons of oil-free moisturizing lotion.

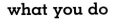 Be careful where you put that slime! If you use food coloring, it'll stain, and it's impossible to get out of carpeting. Don't forget to store it in an airtight container!

Slime Games

Create slime with your friends and play these games. You can all make the same slime, or have each friend make a different recipe and test them out against each other.

Slime Splat

Take turns dropping your slime from your upstairs bedroom window. Ask a sibling to judge which slime had the best splatter. Make sure you put down some plastic garbage bags for your slime to fall on. Don't litter!

Slime Race

Create a downhill track for your slimes, and race against the clock or against each other.

Slime Scientist

Play with the proportion of laundry booster and white glue to see what happens to your slime creation.

Slime Chute

Cut the bottoms off a few 2-liter soda bottles, have contestants hold the bottles upside down, and place their slime in the bottles. The slime that drops through the bottle opening and splats on the ground first wins.

Fetid Fish and Putrid Pickle Phewfume

Perfume was invented to disguise the disgusting smells of unwashed bodies. (See page 68.) Make this perfume to disguise the inoffensive odor of a well-washed body.

what you need

Fish sauce*
Tablespoon
2 small plastic spray bottles
Funnel
Garlic-dill pickle juice or sauerkraut
(the kind that is sold in the refrigerator
section of gross-ery stores)
Strainer
*available in Asian markets

what you do

1 To make the fetid fish phewfume, funnel 2 tablespoons of the fish sauce into a spray bottle.

2 Fill the bottle with water. Put the spray nozzle back on and shake it well.

3 To make the putrid pickle phewfume, strain 4 tablespoons of the pickle juice to remove small particles. Funnel the juice into the second spray bottle.

4 Fill the bottle with water. Put the spray nozzle back on and shake it well.

Dung Beetle Sludge Globe

Lots of people collect and display paperweights that contain pretty things, like the Eiffel Tower surrounded by pure white snowflakes. Yuck. Make this disgusting paperweight for your best gross friend.

what you need

1 ounce each of dark brown and light brown polymer clay
Clear 8-ounce jar with a lid
Aluminum foil
Cookie sheet
Oven
Oven mitts
Plastic dung beetle

Hot glue gun with glue sticks
Water
Green food coloring
1 teaspoon of liquid glycerin*
Mineral oil
Silicone sealant

*Available at drugstores

Get an adult to help you with the oven and the glue.

what you do

1 Squeeze and knead the dark brown polymer clay until you can roll it into a snake. Fold the snake a few times, roll it out, and fold again. Continue rolling and folding the clay until it's soft and warm.

2 Repeat step 1 with the light brown polymer clay. When it's soft and warm, combine the two colors and mix them together a bit.

3 Shape the polymer clay into a 3-inch-long log. Squash and shape the polymer clay into a poop ball that is about 1 inch smaller in diameter than the lid of the jar.

4 Cover the cookie sheet with the foil. Place the poop ball on it, and bake it at 250°F for 20 minutes. Take it out of the oven, and let it cool.

5 When the poop is completely cool, glue the dung beetle onto it with a small dab of the hot glue.

6 Glue the poop onto the underside of the lid with another small glob of the hot glue.

7 Pour about ½ inch of water into the jar. Add 5 or 6 drops of the food coloring to give the water a nice green tint. Then add the glycerin. This keeps the oil from breaking up into tiny bubbles.

8 Add the mineral oil to the jar with the water, leaving enough room at the top of the jar so that when you put the lid on the jar the water doesn't overflow.

9 Apply the silicone sealant in a thick, even line around the inside edge of the lid.

10 Screw the lid onto the jar. Leave the sludge globe alone for several hours to give the sealant time to set.

11 Gently shake the globe to make the sludge cover the dung pile.

Dead Bug Bowl

Morning everyone. Time for breakfast. And I can't think of a better way to start off your morning than finding a bunch of dead bugs at the bottom of your cereal bowl.

what you need

Color pictures of bugs
Tape
Piece of paper
Color photocopier*
Water slide decal paper**
Ceramic bowl (clean and dry)
Scissors

Shallow bowl
Paper towels
Soft, dry cloth
Oven

*Ask your parents if they have one at work, or go to your nearest photocopy center.

**See page 109 for ordering information.

what you do

1 Tape all of your gross bug pictures onto a single sheet of paper. Take it to a photocopying center, and have a color copy made on the shiny side of the water slide decal paper. If someone helps you, ask them to set the toner density on high before photocopying it.

2 With the scissors, carefully cut around all the images on the water slide decal paper.

3 Figure out where you want the images to go in the ceramic bowl.

4 To apply the images, fill the shallow bowl with luke warm water. Put the first image facedown in the bowl. Let it soak until the paper rolls up slightly and gets more see-through.

5 Very, very carefully take the image out of the water. Blot it gently with the paper towel to remove some of the excess water. Carefully slide one corner of the image off the backing paper.

6 Put the image, faceup, on the bowl where you want it to go. Gently hold it in place with one hand while you slide the backing paper out from underneath it.

7 Rub the soft, dry cloth over the image very gently, working from the inside to all the edges. This will remove any air bubbles or creases.

8 Repeat steps 4 through 7 until all of the images are on the bowl.

9 Let the bowl sit for at least 24 hours. Then, get an adult to bake it in the oven at 350°F for 10 minutes. This will make the images melt and harden onto the bowl, so they won't ever come off. You can wash the bowl, but don't put it in the dishwasher.

Goopy Booger Bath Soap

Imagine bathing with soap that looks and feels just like those yogurt-textured snots that you hack up from the back of your throat when you have a bad cold. You can use this stuff as liquid hand soap, or put it in your bath for a gross way to clean, healthy skin. Great gift for teacher!

what you need

Measuring cup and spoons
¼ cup grated clear glycerin melt-and-pour soap base*
Glass bowl
Microwave
¼ cup clear aloe vera gel**
¼ cup witch hazel**
3 tablespoons liquid glycerin**

Spoon
Package of unsweetened lemon or lime powdered drink mix
8-ounce plastic container

*Available at the soapmaking supply department of craft stores
**Available at drugstores

Get an adult to help you melt and pour the soap!

what you do

1 Place the grated soap in the glass bowl, and heat it in the microwave for 30 seconds. Keep melting the soap in 15-second intervals until it's completely liquid. Don't let the soap overheat or boil.

2 Remove the melted soap from the microwave, and gently stir in the aloe vera gel, the witch hazel, and the glycerin. Don't stir it too vigorously, or you'll get bubbles.

3 Sprinkle in the lemon or lime powdered drink mix a little at a time. Stir the soap after each addition, and quit when you get the perfect booger color.

4 Transfer the boogers into the plastic container. Let the boogers sit undisturbed for three or four hours so that they congeal. Tie a ribbon around the container, and give it to someone you love.

When Things Were Rotten

Wanna hear something really gross? Of course you do. Believe it or not, back in the olden days in most of Europe, bathing was considered bad for your health. In fact, if you took a bath once in your life, you were one up on most of the rest of your neighbors. Now, before you step in that time machine hoping to go back to a better, simpler, grosser time, read on. In the 16th century, people believed that there was a layer of oil covering your skin that kept diseases from getting in. They figured bathing would wash away the oil and they'd get sick. They had it backward, of course, and in fact, convincing a whole town, city, or even country not to bathe is a great way to set off a plague or two. So much for the good ol' days.

Royal Stinkers

Queen Isabel of Spain boasted that she only bathed twice in her life—once when she was born and once before she was married.

King Louis XII also only took two baths in his life.

Almost 100 years later, Queen Elizabeth I of England made a habit of bathing once every three months (whether she needed it or not)!

King Louis XIV frequently held court in France while sitting on his own personal throne, doing his royal business. It was considered a great honor to speak with the King while he relieved himself.

Henry IV smelled so much like rotten meat, his bride swooned when she first saw (or rather smelled) him.

Shrunken Head

Ralph and Betty Lou wanted to put a REAL shrunken head in this book. I convinced them that this would be a suitable substitution. Plus it's much easier to find an apple than it is to find a head.

what you need

Apple
Vegetable peeler
Long, sharp pencil
Butter knife

Pushpins or thumbtacks
Grains of uncooked rice
Nespaper
Mug or cup

what you do

1 Peel the skin off the apple. Twist and push the pencil into the bottom of the apple until it's about halfway through it.

2 With an adult, carve a nose, mouth, and two eye sockets with the knife. Then stick a pushpin or thumbtack into each socket.

3 Stick grains of rice into the mouth for teeth. Crumple up some newspaper and put it in the bottom of the mug. Stick the pencil part of the apple head in the middle. Be sure that the apple itself doesn't touch the rim or the cup at all.

4 Let the apple head air-dry in a dry place for about two weeks or until it shrivels into a weird, wrinkly head!

A Mummy for Mommy

The ancient Egyptians perfected the art of mummification. Follow in their footsteps with this project.

what you need

Whole chicken
Towel
Lots of salt
Baking soda
Cloth bag
Gallon-sized, resealable
   plastic bag (big
   enough to hold
   the entire chicken)
Smaller resealable
   plastic bags (optional)

Olive oil
Rosemary, cinnamon,
   and cloves
White craft glue
Water
Bowl
Linen or cloth,
   torn into strips

Um...make sure your parents know what you're going to do with the chicken, and keep your mummy away from pets and out of bedrooms. And, wash your hands well after you've handled the chicken.

what you do

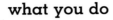

1 Remove all of the chicken's internal organs. You can mummify them too if you want. The Egyptians did—except for the brain, which they sucked out of the nose with a straw. They threw it away because they thought it was worthless. Don't worry about your chicken's brain. It's too small to affect the mummification process at all. Set the organs aside if you want to mummify them as well.

2 Wash the chicken, inside and out. Blot off the extra water with the towel.

3 Mix together a whole bunch of equal parts salt and baking soda. The chemical composition of this mixture is the closest you can get to *natron*, the salt the Egyptians used, without going to the Nile to collect it yourself.

4 Fill the cloth bag with the salt and baking soda mixture. Put it inside the chicken.

5 Put the chicken in the plastic bag. Pour more of the salt and baking soda mixture into the bag so the chicken is completely covered, and seal it. If you want to mummify the chicken's organs, put them in separate, smaller resealable plastic bags, and fill them with the salt and baking soda mixture.

6 Check on the chicken every four or five days to see how well it's drying out. The salt and baking soda mixture will absorb the water from the body. Change it when it gets moist. Don't forget to change the salt and baking soda inside the chicken too. It will take about four to six weeks, so be patient. Keep changing the salt and baking soda mixture!

(There's more mummy on the next page.)

Mummy for Mommy continued

7 You'll know the chicken is dry when it doesn't stink anymore. Take it out of the bag, and rub off all the salt. (Don't **wash** the salt off, whatever you do. You'll have to start the drying process all over again.) If you've mummified the internal organs of the chickens, they'll still stink. They always will.

8 Rub the olive oil into the chicken.

9 Rub the rosemary, cinnamon, and cloves into the chicken.

10 Mix together equal parts of the white craft glue and water in a small bowl.

11 Wrap the chicken with the strips of cloth. Dip each one in the glue mixture, coating it evenly. Then wrap it around the chicken. Keep wrapping it until the oil doesn't soak through anymore.

12 If you've mummified the internal organs, place them in clear jars with lids so everybody can see how gross they are.

The completed mummy and the organs on display make perfect Mummy's Day gifts!

Putrid Paper

Here's a handy recipe for making your own putrid paper with dead insects in it. You won't find this sickening stationery at any local store! What a perfect present for your putrid pen pal.

what you need

Light-colored scrap paper
  (1 cup per sheet of paper
  you wish to make)
Piece of metal window screen
Tin snips for cutting screen*
Water
Measuring cup
Blender

Dishpan or washtub
Dead bugs
2 pieces of thick wool felt
  larger than the size of paper
Rolling pin
Laundry line and clothespins

* You only need tin snips if your screen
   is too big for the dishpan.

what you do

1 Rip up the light-colored scrap paper into 1-inch squares. You can use all different kinds of paper, except really dark paper or newsprint.

2 Use the tin snips to cut the screen to the size of paper you want to make. (A regular notebook sheet is 8½ x 11 inches.) Set the screen aside.

3 Put a handful of paper scraps in the blender. Cover them with about 1½ cups of water. Let them soak for a bit.

4 Blend your concoction until it looks sort of like watery oatmeal. Keep adding handfuls of scrap to the mixture, and turn the blender off and on in short bursts to chop it up. If your mixture is too watery, add some more paper. If it's too thick, add some more water. (More putridness on the following page.)

5 Pour the pulp into the dishpan, until you have about 5 inches of it.

6 Slide the window screen under the water to collect the pulp on it. Move it back and forth until the pulp settles evenly across the surface of the screen.

7 Pull the screen straight up. Let the water run through the screen so that just the pulp stays on the surface level. It should be about ½ inch thick. If your paper looks like it's too thin, add more pulp to the dishpan, and dip the screen again. If it seems too thick, add some water to the dishpan, and re-dip the screen.

8 Put the screen on your work surface. Artfully arrange dead bugs on the surface of the paper. Gently press them into the pulp so that they are partially covered. Be careful not to bury them completely, although they do need to have some pulp covering them so they'll stick to the paper.

9 To squeeze the water out of the paper, lay one of your felt sheets down on your work surface. Put the screen pulp side down on the felt, and cover it with the other layer of felt.

10 Roll the rolling pin evenly back and forth across the felt to get out the extra water and mash together the fibers of the paper.

11 Gently peel the felt layers off the sheet of paper. Go slowly here so you don't rip the wet paper.

12 Clip your new paper to a laundry line (or anywhere that's warm and dry if it's raining outside), and let it dry for about three hours.

Finding dead bugs is easy if you know where to look! Check inside light fixtures (unplug them first!) and on windowsills. You should find more bugs than you could possibly use.

Lose-Your-Lunch Locker Magnet

This awesome magnet will remind "Blow-Chunk" Charlie of the time he delivered a pavement pizza during recess in third grade. He'll appreciate it, and it might inspire a future performance or two.

what you need

Polymer clay in green, pink, yellow, and brown
Plastic rolling pin or acrylic rod

Butter knife
Cookie sheet
Oven
Self-adhesive magnet

what you do

1 Squeeze and knead the green polymer clay until you can roll it into a snake. Fold the snake a few times, roll it out, and fold again. Continue rolling and folding the clay until it's soft and warm. (This is called conditioning the clay, and if you don't condition it, your finished project may break.)

2 Repeat step 1 with the pink, yellow, and brown polymer clay. These colors will be the chunks in your upchuck, so you won't need too much of this clay.

3 Roll the green polymer clay out into a sheet about ¼ inch thick with the rolling pin or acrylic rod.

4 Cut around the edges of the green sheet of polymer clay with the butter knife, making it look like a puddle of vomit.

5 Tear off small chunks of the pink, yellow, and brown polymer clay. Gently place them on and in the green vomit base.

6 Preheat the oven to 275°F. Put the vomit on the cookie sheet, and bake it for 20 to 30 minutes.

7 Take out the vomit, and let it cool completely. Stick the self-adhesive magnet to the back.

Revolting Wrapping Paper

Presentation is always important—especially if you're giving somebody a gift that you made. Make a disgusting stamp, use it to decorate some old paper, and tah-dah! A truly gross present you can be proud of.

what you need

Kitchen knife
Potato
Black felt-tipped pen
Paring knife

Ink pad
Brown craft paper (or any other blank paper)

Make sure an adult helps you with the cutting.

what you do

1 Cut the potato in half lengthwise with the kitchen knife.

2 Draw something disgusting on the inside of the potato with the felt-tipped pen. Color in the part that will be the stamp.

3 Cut away the flesh of the potato around the stamp. Make sure it's about ¼ inch lower than the part of the potato that will be the stamp.

4 Ink the stamp by placing it gently on the stamp pad. Put the stamp on the brown craft paper and stamp it. Do it again. And again.

5 Let the ink dry. When it's dry, wrap one of your gross gifts in it, and give it to your friend.

CHAPTER FOUR

The Gross Outdoors

Ah...the gross outdoors. The hot sun beating down, speeding up the process of decay everywhere. Swarms of flies landing on my peanut butter and jelly sandwich, knowing that they're eating my food, throwing it up, and sucking it up again, leaving all sorts of germs behind. Maggots gnawing their way through the corpse of a small, dead, furry animal. Just knowing that somewhere, along a quiet two-lane highway, there's a vulture tearing at the intestines of some roadkill makes me glad to be alive. Ah...I can just smell it now.... What!? You don't know about the gross outdoors! Well, you better get reading. There's a lot for you to learn. Get going already. The slugs, maggots, and corpse flowers are waiting for you.

Big Fun Fungus

Mold is a form of fungus, like a mushroom: neither plant, nor animal. Pretty creepy, eh!? Fungi don't produce their own food. Instead, they suck it out of the living or dead things they grow on.

what you need

Bread

Fruit

Veggies

Cheese

Water

Glass jar with lid

what you do

1 Put the bread, fruit, veggies, and cheese in the glass jar.

2 Artfully arrange them, then sprinkle a few drops of water into the jar.

3 Put the lid on the jar, and seal it tightly. Place the jar in a warm, dark location.

4 Wait for the mold to start growing. Check on it every few days. When your mold garden has lots of different beautiful molds growing on it, give it to someone as a special token of their grossness.

The biggest living thing on Earth is a fungus. It's in Washington State, USA, and takes up more than 2½ square miles.

Slime: The Real Deal

The gross outdoors is a great place for finding slimy stuff. There are slugs, snails, and slime mold! Slime mold is an orange glob of, well, slime. It can move! It crawls along dead trees and logs, eating the bacteria that live on the surface.

You can find slime mold living on an old rotting log, or you can grow your own.

what you need

Agar* (that's a growth nutrient)
Measuring spoons
Petri dish**
Physarum polycephalum*
   (that's slime mold!)

Knife
Oatmeal flakes

*See page 109 for information on ordering slime kits.
**Available at science supply stores and some school supply stores

what you do

1 Put ½ teaspoon of agar into the petri dish.

2 Cut a small piece off the physarum polycephalum. (Don't worry, you won't hurt it.) Put it upside down in the petri dish.

3 Put two or three oatmeal flakes in the dish, about an inch away from the slime.

4 Put the lid on the petri dish, and go do something else. Come back and look at the slime the next day. It will have probably grown over the oatmeal flakes.

5 Every day, feed another few flakes of oatmeal to the slime mold. In a few days, the oatmeal will turn into something really gross.

Munchin' Maggots

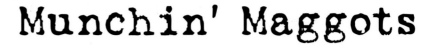

Newborn maggots (baby flies) are hatched in stinky garbage cans, rotting animal flesh, or just about anywhere else that's rancid. They eat all sorts of stuff: leftover food, rotting garbage, oozing sores, stinky poop...the grosser it is, the better. Here's how you can make your own maggot nursery.

what you need

Banana
Jar

Nylon stocking
Rubber band

what you do

1 Peel the banana. Put it in the jar, and turn the jar on its side. Leave it in a shady location for about three days.

2 Look at the banana every day. When you see five to 10 fruit flies in the jar, slip the nylon stocking over the opening in the jar. Secure it with the rubber band.

3 Hold the fruit flies hostage for three days. Then, remove the nylon and release them. Replace the nylon.

4 Watch the jar for the next two weeks. In a few days, you'll start to see maggots crawling around on the banana. Watch them wiggle! Watch them squirm! Watch them dig! After the baby maggots grow up a little bit, they'll turn into small white capsules. Then, new fruit flies will emerge. Let them go outside away from the house. Throw away the jar and what's left of the banana.

Maggot Medicine

Back before modern medicine, if you had a festering, infected wound, your doctor may have had the perfect remedy: a handful of maggots placed in your wound. Before you scream, "Get my lawyer!", check this out. Maggots would eat the dead, rotting, and disgusting skin and flesh in your big boo boo, leaving behind a substance that actually helped clean the wound. That stuff is called *allotoin*, and it's a natural antiseptic, and not too different from the antibiotics doctors use today. How does one get rid of the creepy crawly bugs once they're in your wound? You simply wait for them to turn into flies and take off. By the way, maggot medicine is making a comeback. Some doctors today have started using maggots again for people allergic to antibiotics.

Our Special Guest Star Interview: The Cockroach

Ralph: So Mr. Cockroach, I fart about 40 times a day. How 'bout you?

Cockroach: Well, Ralph, I usually fart about four times an hour. Got ya beat there.

Ralph: I heard you could walk around for a week without your head.

Cockroach: I hope never to find out if that's true.

Ralph: Why do cockroaches have such bad reputations? I mean, you guys have been around for about 350 million years. You're older than dinosaurs, for gosh sakes. That's an awful lot of time to hire a P.R. firm.

Cockroach: Well, I can think of a few things. For instance, there's my cousin in Brazil that feeds exclusively on eyelashes.

Ralph: Cool.

Cockroach: Oh, yeah, and even though people used to give us as housewarming presents, we're very difficult to kill; we can slip through paper thin cracks. Did you know that invisible piles of cockroach poop are terrible health hazards, especially for people who suffer from asthma?

We'll eat just about anything, even sweaty sneakers, TV wires, fingernails, other cockroaches, soap, whatever. We like to throw dances on your dirty dishes in your kitchen at night. And speaking just for myself, I have about 10 million kids, and most of them live under your bed as we speak.

Ralph: Cool.

Cockroach: Oh, and one more—we like to slither into ears.

The Dung Beetle Farm

Got an ant farm? Evict the ants and rent to the dung beetles. They're awesome tenants. They clean up after themselves, and best of all, they eat cow poop.

what you need

Ant farm
Fine soil
Leaf litter
Dung beetle
Dung*

*Make sure your dung comes from herbivores. Cow or sheep dung is best!

what you do

1 Set up your ant farm. If it came with ants, get rid of them.

2 Fill it with the fine soil and the leaf litter. Don't forget to leave about 5 inches of empty space at the top of the dung beetle farm.

3 Get a dung beetle. You can order one on the Internet (see page 109), or you can simply go to a local farm that has cows or sheep and pick up some dung. The beetles are in there, for sure.

4 Put the dung beetle in its new home. Add some fresh dung.

A Day at the Slug Races

Imagine the excitement! The slime! The tentacles! Yes, ladies and gentlemen, it's time for the slug races.

what you need

1 slug for each slug jockey (you and your friends)
Piece of clear, hard plastic sheeting*
4 chairs to prop the plastic sheeting up on
Salt

*The most common version of this is Plexiglas.

what you do

1 Each slug jockey must find a slug. Slugs look a lot like snails, but without the shell, and they like to hang out in dark, moist, disgusting places. Look under rotting logs and flip over rocks, or create a slug trap by covering some wet grass in your yard with plastic sheeting or an old board. Wait several days, then grab some slugs.

2 Place the four edges of the plastic sheeting on top of the chairs. Make sure that there's enough room beneath the plastic sheeting for each slug jockey.

3 Create lanes for each slug by adding lines of salt from the start to finish lines. Slugs don't like salt and will avoid the lines.

4 Line up the slugs on one side of the plastic sheeting. Make sure they're all pointing in the same direction. Shout "Go!" (This is more for the contestant's sake than the slugs. They don't really care about you or your dreams of winning the National Gastropod Championship.)

(The race continues on page 90.)

A Day at the Slug Races continued

5 Slug jockeys may not tap on the plastic sheeting, tilt it, or mess with the slugs in any way. This is their moment to slime (I mean shine!), so back off!

6 The first slug to make it to the other side of the plastic sheeting wins! Losers have to lick the slime off the plastic sheeting. Hee, hee.

Imagine what you'd look like if you only had one foot, no arms, eyes on two tentacles, and a breathing hole in your side. Know what you'd be? A no-armed-one-footed-breathing-through-your-side-tentacle-eyed-human. Or a *gastropod*, which is Latin for "stomach-foot." Some gastropods have shells, like snails, others do not. The one thing they all have in common is that they've only got one foot. A gastropod's foot is one big muscle that kind of creeps along. That's probably why they move so slowly. Their slime helps them slide along on that foot.

The Most Fun Activity in This Whole Book

Touch a slug.

Why?
Because it's GROSS!

Grow a Poop Plant

Yes, that humble piece of bird poop that just landed on Ralph can grow into a beautiful plant...but only if you give it just the right amount of love.

what you need

Bird poop (don't touch it)
Trowel (that's a mini shovel)
Weed-free dirt
Paper
Pen
Glue
Craft stick
Watering can

what you do

1 Find a piece of bird poop. Use the trowel to scrape it off whatever it's glued itself to.

2 Plant the bird poop somewhere weed-free. Cover it with about 2 inches of soil.

3 Make a sign for the poop plant. Write its name on the paper with the pen and glue it to the craft stack. Let the glue dry.

(More on Poop Plants on page 92.)

The Gross Outdoors **91**

Grow a Poop Plant continued

4 Stick the sign into the ground by the bird poop so you can remember where it is.

5 Water the soil around the bird poop. Check on the spot every day. Make sure the soil stays evenly moist, but not completely soaked.

6 In a few weeks, if the poop had seeds in it, the poop plant will start to grow up out of the ground.

Birds plant lots of seeds. Plants hide their seeds in delicious fruits and berries for the birds to eat. The birds eat the seeds along with the fruit. Then, the seeds pass through the bird's digestive track and are planted with a nice coating of organic materials. There are some seeds, like tomato and blackberry seeds, that cannot sprout until they've gone through somebody's digestive system.

Killer Plants

Carnivorous plants eat insects, and some even catch mice and small birds. You'd think these plants would get pretty hungry, considering that their prey can move and they can't. But they have developed ways of bringing their dinner to them.

Many stores now sell carnivorous plants, so you can make your own death-terrarium.

what you need

5-gallon glass or clear
  plastic container
Gravel
Bucket
Distilled water
Peat moss
Sand

Spoon
A nice selection of
  carnivorous plants
Cup or watering can
Wooden block or
  other weight

what you do

1 Clean and dry your container. Spread a ½-inch layer of gravel on the bottom.

2 Holding a clump of peat moss in your hand, submerge it in the bucket of distilled water, and squeeze all the air out of it. This helps the peat absorb and retain water.

3 Mix together the wet peat and sand in a 2 to 1 ratio, that is, 2 cups of peat to 1 cup of sand. Spread a 2- to 3-inch layer of the mix over the gravel. In the wild, carnivorous plants live in bogs with extremely poor soil, so don't add any fertilizer, or you'll kill the plants.

(More on the next page.)

Killer Plants continued

4 Use the spoon to carefully dig holes in the layer of peat and sand. Position the plants in the holes, one plant in each. Gently fill in the holes around the plants with more peat mixture, covering their roots.

5 Use the cup or watering can to gently sprinkle 1 or 2 cups of distilled water inside the terrarium. Don't use tap water because it contains minerals harmful to the plants. Carnivorous plants like air with a high humidity level, so always keep the soil moist but not soupy. Don't close up the container, or you'll end up growing fungus instead of killer plants.

6 Put your terrarium on a windowsill where it will get bright light. (Facing south is the best.) Use the wooden block or weight to keep the container from moving.

7 To feed your plants, you can put small bits of raw steak on the end of a toothpick, and gently touch it inside the plant's jaws. Or, help attract flies to the terrarium by putting a sugar cube inside the jar. Wait until a fly flies in, and watch the feast begin!

Stop to Smell the Awfully Disgusting Flowers

The rafflesia flower is the stinkiest, nastiest, grossest flower on Earth. It is also known as the corpse flower, because that's exactly what it smells like. The smell of rotting meat attracts the insects that fertilize it. The rafflesia flower grows in the rain forests of southeast Asia. A single bloom can be 3 feet across—that's enough flower to create one huge stink!

Tour the Gross Zoo

Sure we probably look and act gross to a bunch of the animals out there. (Hey, most of us pick our noses, and some of us even eat it.) But here are some animals that are just plain old foul, no matter how you look at them. Come, follow me!

Exhibition #1: One out of every five living things is a beetle.

Exhibition #2: Slime eels are completely covered in the mucus they secrete out of their 90 slime pores. If you get slimed, you have to pull the stuff off. The mucus just gets thicker in water. To eat, slime eels slither along the ocean floor until they come across a dead or dying fish. They slither into the animal, through the mouth, eye, butt, or any other opening, and then eat it from the inside out.

Exhibition #3: Jellyfish. They're squishy, slimy, and eat and pee out of the same hole. No wonder they have no brains.

(The Tour continues on page 96.)

Tour the Gross Zoo continued

Exhibition #4: Rabbits may look all cute and cuddly, but baby rabbits have to eat their own poop to stay healthy.

Exhibition #5: The Frigate Bird chases other birds and forces them to throw up their meal. It then eats the vomited-up food. How's that for take-out food?

Exhibition #6: Geckos can lick their own eyeballs.

Exhibition #7: A type of African Mongoose has a butt that looks like a flower. As soon as an insect lands, the Mongoose whips around and chomps it up.

Exhibition #8: Vicious Blue Fish attack schools of fish on the Eastern coast of North America. They kill more than 10 times the number of fish they can eat, devour up 40 at a time, and then puke them up so they can keep eating.

Exhibition #9: The Naked Mole-Rat has no hair except inside its mouth. You can see the inside of a naked mole-rat when it's first born: the skin is translucent!

Exhibition #10: A toad or frog pushes its eyeballs back in its head to help it swallow.

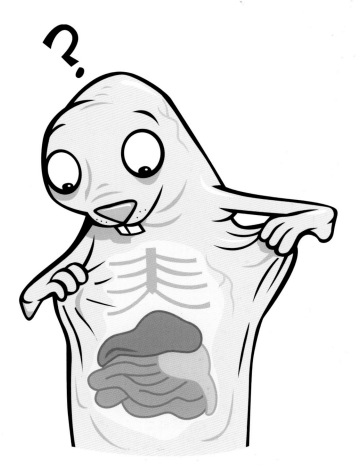

Sickening Scavenger Hunt

Turn off the TV. Stop playing video games. Get outside, and find some gross stuff.

what you need

Paper
Pens
Shovels
Shoeboxes
Some friends

what you do

1 Come up with a list of disgusting things you can find in your backyard or when you're on your next camping trip. Here are some to get you started:

Spittlebugs: They live on leafy weeds or grasses in fields or woods. The spittlebug babies (*nymphs* if you must) make frothy nests that look like a huge, bubbly lougie.

Slime mold

Fungus

Slugs

Stinkbugs

Bird poop (don't touch)

Dead animals (don't touch)

Centipedes or millipedes

Worms

2 Once everyone has the same list in hand, say, "Go!", or something like that, and start searching. Collect all the gross stuff you can find. The first person who returns with a shoebox filled with everything wins. What does that person win? What's in everyone else's box, of course.

CHAPTER FIVE

You're Gross and You're Proud

You've explored your gross body and dug deeper than anyone dreamed for that extra bit of belly button lint. You burped the alphabet BACKWARDS. You dined with Gross Grandma and lived to boast about it. You showered your family and friends with gifts that kept them gagging. And finally, you traveled the four corners of Earth (okay, the four corners of your yard) searching for all that is gross. It's official. You're a Grosstranaut. Your certificate is on page 107. Fill it out. Hang it up. Whatever. As a Grosstranaut, it will be your job to uphold all the gross traditions, and explore and push the boundaries of grossness. Gotta fart? Make sure there's a little kid around to pull your finger. Need a pet? Find one that rolls perfectly perfect poop balls. When people run screaming away from something hideously gross that manages to offend all five senses at once, you're there, ready to take a picture. Hold your head up high (unless you're looking for gross bugs or toe jam), and read the following pages to complete your training. Congratulations. We knew you could do it.

Grosstranaut slogan:

One small step for gross kids…one giant leap for grosskind.

Grosstranaut Sing-along

As a proud member of the Grosstranauts, you'll need to learn our song. Sing it loud and often. Belch it if you can.

To the tune of "The 12 Days of Christmas":
If you don't know the song, any old tune you've got stuck in your head will do.

On the first day of Gross-Out Day my gross friend gave to me: a gaseous gift that smells like rotten eggs.

On the second day of Gross-Out Day, my gross friend gave to me: two booger balls, and a gaseous gift that smells like rotten eggs.

On the third day of Gross-Out Day, my gross friend gave to me: three vials of vomit, two booger balls, and a gaseous gift that smells like rotten eggs.

On the fourth day of Gross-Out Day, my gross friend gave to me: four mounds of maggots, etc.

On the fifth day of Gross-Out Day, my gross friend gave to me: five jars of toe jam, etc.

On the sixth day of Gross-Out Day, my gross friend gave to me: six pus-filled roadkill sandwiches, etc.

On the seventh day of Gross-Out Day, my gross friend gave to me: seven diarrhea diapers, etc.

On the eighth day of Gross-Out Day, my gross friend gave to me: eight edible eyeballs, etc.

On the ninth day of Gross-Out Day, my gross friend gave to me: nine ear wax candles, etc.

Question:
When's Gross Out Day, anyway?

Answer:
EVERY DAY,
of course!

On the tenth day of Gross-Out Day, my gross friend gave to me: 10 green toenail clippings (from 1992), etc.

On the eleventh day of Gross-Out Day my gross friend gave to me: 11 pairs of my dad's black socks (unwashed, of course), etc.

On the twelfth day of Gross-Out Day, my gross friend gave to me: 12 dookie donuts, etc.

Make up your own version if you want!

Gross Games

Here are a bunch of games we play at Grosstranaut get-togethers. Great for recruiting new Grosstranauts.

Gross Picnic

Gather a bunch of friends together right before dinner. Sit in a circle, and tell them that you're going on a gross picnic, and you're going to bring…now name something really gross that begins with the letter A, such as Ant Intestine Sandwich. The person to your right then repeats "I'm going on a gross picnic, and I'm gonna bring…and that person says something gross that begins with B, such as Barf Bag Bile Banana Pudding. Go around the circle, and keep going until you get through the alphabet. If you don't get any groans or looks of horror from the other players when it's your turn, you have to try again.

Cola Roulette

Get a six-pack of cola (something really fizzy), and six players. Shake one can of cola furiously, and then, mix the cans up. Have each player pick up a can, and put it up to his nose. On the count of three, each player opens his can. Once again, everyone wins this game, although one player gets fizzy cola up his nose.

Yogurt Mess

Each player puts a new pair of nylon stockings over his head, completely covering his mouth. On the count of three, each player opens a small container of fruity yogurt and starts eating. Spoons optional. With this game, there are no losers.

SPIZZZSH!

Broken Egg Relay Race

This is just like a regular relay race, except that instead of passing a baton to your relay partners, you're passing an egg yolk. If you drop your yolk, you lose. The first team to cross the finish line with most of the yolk intact wins.

Gross Eating Contest

At the next party, pick two teams and have the teams sit across from each other. Pick a referee, and have the referee blindfold each player. The referee then goes in the kitchen and fills two paper bags with gross food items that may smell or feel gross. (Don't use spoiled food.) Each bag should contain the same items. The bags could be filled with raw onion pieces, cold beans, chunks of cheese, cold spaghetti, hardboiled eggs, and more! When the referee says, "Go!", the first blindfolded contestant on each team grabs one thing from the bag and eats it. Once the item is swallowed, he passes the bag to the next player, she grabs an item from the bag and eats it, and so on. The first team to finish off the bag, wins.

Play these games outside!

Gross Etiquette

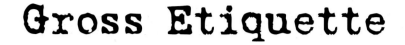

As a grosstranaut, it's your responsibility to remember these simple rules for proper gross behavior.

BRRRRAAAAAPP!

Never blame the dog. Fart loud, be proud.

Belch loud and often.

Always help Gross Grandma cross the street.

Body fart noises are always appropriate.

Show off scabs and lesions at every opportunity and family gathering.

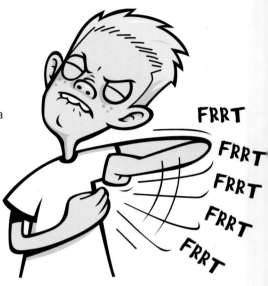

FRRT
FRRT
FRRT
FRRT
FRRT

Only pick your nose in public. Don't eat it unless you have enough for everybody.

Don't leave your toe jam on the floor where you picked it out. Roll it into a ball and save it for later.

Don't keep all your disgusting craft ideas, recipes, facts, and trivia to yourself. Share.

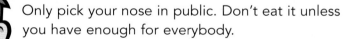

BL'S BOOGER BAG

Congratulations! Grosstranaut

Please fill in your name below to complete your training.

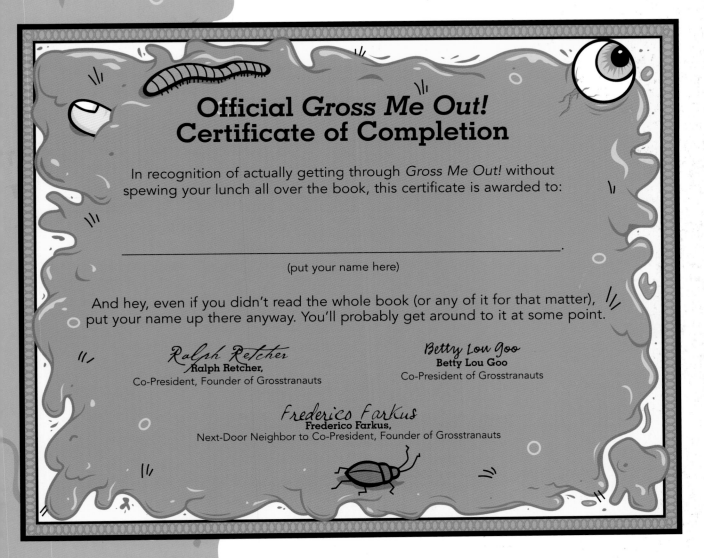

Official *Gross Me Out!* Certificate of Completion

In recognition of actually getting through *Gross Me Out!* without spewing your lunch all over the book, this certificate is awarded to:

_____.

(put your name here)

And hey, even if you didn't read the whole book (or any of it for that matter), put your name up there anyway. You'll probably get around to it at some point.

Ralph Retcher
Ralph Retcher,
Co-President, Founder of Grosstranauts

Betty Lou Goo
Betty Lou Goo
Co-President of Grosstranauts

Frederico Farkus
Frederico Farkus,
Next-Door Neighbor to Co-President, Founder of Grosstranauts

Metric Conversion

Inches	Centimeters
⅛	3 mm
¼	6 mm
⅜	9 mm
½	1.3
⅝	1.6
¾	1.9
⅞	2.2
1	2.5
1¼	3.1
1½	3.8
1¾	4.4
2	5
2½	6.3
3	7.5
3½	8.8
4	10
4½	11.3
5	12.5
5½	13.8
6	15
7	17.5
8	20
9	22.5
10	25
11	27.5
12	30

To convert inches to centimeters, multiply by 2.54

To convert liquid cups to milliliters, first multiply the cups by 8 to get ounces, then multiply by 30

To convert dry cups to milliliters, first multiply the cups by 8 to get ounces, then multiply by 28

To convert teaspoons to milliliters, multiply by 5

To convert tablespoons to milliliters, multiply by 15

To convert ounces to milliliters, multiply by 30

To convert quarts to liters, multiply by 0.95

To convert gallons to liters, multiply by 3.8

To convert pounds to kilograms, multiply by 0.454

To convert Fahrenheit temperatures to Celsius, subtract 32, then multiply by 5/9

A Note About Suppliers

Most of the supplies you need for making the projects in this book can be found at your local craft store, discount mart, or home improvement center. However, you may need to find some materials (like dung beetles) from specialists. In order to provide you with the most up-to-date information, check out the suppliers' list on our Web site. Visit us at www.larkbooks.com, click on "Craft Supply Sources," and then click on the relevant topic. You'll find several companies that can help you get what you need. They're listed with their web address and/or mailing address and phone number.

Acknowledgments

Books this disgusting can't be created without lots of help from our gross friends. In particular, we'd like to thank: **Clay Meyer,** illustrator extraordinaire and lover of all things gross, for the hard work and late nights; **Stacey Budge,** who spent a lot of time studying the color of snot, spit, and bile to get every page perfect; the kids who taught us the proper method for achieving the perfect fake fart noise and showed us that it's impossible to be too gross: **Chance Barry, Mariella Buddle, Tyler Pratt,** and **Chelsea Wise; Allison Smith,** who designed a bunch of the projects for this book, and to her children for their enthusiasm and advice along the way; **Janice Eaton Kilby,** Queen of All Things Repugnant, who came up with the idea for this book in the first place; **Nicole Tuggle** for sharing her truly unique library of extremely gross books; and last, but certainly not least, thanks to all of our co-workers who managed (barely) to hold onto their lunches while this book was in progress.

Index
(Your guide to finding everything gross in this book.)

Got something gross to share with us? We want to hear all about it. Hey, if it's gross enough, we'll even put it in our next book (if they let us do one, that is). Send us an e-mail at kids@larkbooks.com, or some snail mail at Kids at Lark, Lark Books, 67 Broadway, Asheville, NC, 28801. But please don't send us your mummified chickens. Those are for your mummy. (Besides, we already have a whole crypt full.)

BRRRRAAAAPP!

That's it, we're finished here…but your journey has just begun. Good luck, Grosstranaut. May the Fart Be With You.